I0464055

Righteous

Capitalism

by Ian G. Spong

Righteous Capitalism

For many people capitalism has become a pariah, a bad word, but is that primarily because they have a narrow definition of capitalism? Is there a broader definition that includes righteous capitalism? That is what this book is about.

Does theology have any contribution to make towards economics, business and government policies? Do the financial principles, the business models and government legislation of ancient Israel and the teachings of New Testament Christianity play a role today in solving world financial problems? That is also what this book is all about.

Righteous Capitalism

Contents

Righteous Capitalism

Righteous Capitalism

Capitalism

To understand righteous capitalism, must we not first understand capital?

When someone says that they are against capitalism, I am tempted to ask them to remove their clothes. Isn't clothing also capital? Isn't the food on our tables and aren't the homes we live in also capital? Capital is sometimes referred to by the income it produces, but a broader definition includes "the money, property and other valuables which collectively represent the wealth of an individual or business"[1]. Aren't people then somewhat ludicrous if they are against all capitalism? Perhaps what they really mean is that they are against greed.

When the boys and girls on television's stock market channels claim that America is the world's last great bastion of free-market capitalism I don't believe them. If we want real free-market capitalism, we must go to some of the dirty back waters of the third world, where capital is free to operate with impunity and complete disregard for pollution or human life. No, in a civilized country like America, the fairy-tale fiction of a free-market is always balanced by the greater responsibility towards society as a whole.

When those same boys and girls claim that America is a capitalist country and Europe is socialist, I also don't believe them, because the real experts in the field of economics call both markets mixed economies.

America and Europe have varying mixtures of government and private capital at work. When some of the same people claim that European models have failed, they only point out Greece and Italy and Spain. They completely ignore our own failures like California and Europe's successes like Germany and Switzerland and Norway, all of which have healthier mixed-market economies in 2012 than America's particular variety of mixed-market capitalism. Silly arguments come from people with blind parochialism and complete lack of experience of living on the economy in Europe.

In this discussion we will use a broader definition of capital than that of those who are really speaking of greed. Capital includes the shirts or blouses on our backs. Under such a definition, even communism was a form of state capitalism (although a perverted kind). Monarchy was a form of capitalism with one large capitalist, privileged sycophants and a large pool of serfs who may have only owned the clothes on their backs and a few personal items. Even Pharaoh is said to have run Egypt like one huge plantation, with himself being the principal overseer and everyone else subservient. Pharaonic capitalism was actually a variety of monarchial capitalism (both my own phrases). In short, all of human history has been one kind of capitalism or another. There have been abundant cases of evil kinds of capitalism and a few shining examples of incredibly good forms of capitalism.

We will also challenge the shallow thinking that if private enterprise engages in business that is capitalism, but if government engages in business that is socialism. In this book we will look at both government and private business as forms of capitalism. We will also look at a curiosity called corporate socialism, a form of socialism engaged in by the private sector. In so doing we will seek to thoroughly expand our minds beyond the simplistic ideas of the news media's propaganda which is aimed at largely ignorant, shallow-thinking masses.

Moral Shades of Capitalism

Why righteous capitalism? The term moral capitalism is simply not good enough for our discussion. Morality changes from generation to generation. It is too inconsistent. For instance, the form of slavery that existed in the southern United States of America was considered to be quite moral by a large portion of the population at the time, even though it existed because of kidnapping in Africa and existing families were often brutally separated. A similar argument could be made regarding our present prison system, but that is a discussion for another day. Our generation considers that early American form of slavery immoral. Righteous capitalism is concerned with absolute standards of morality that do not change from generation to generation.

Kidnapping is always unrighteous. Indentured servitude without hope of release which exists on the basis of an original kidnapping is unrighteous. Enslaving the children and grandchildren of such kidnap victims is unrighteous. Destruction of families for commercial gain is unrighteous. Using such slaves as sex slaves is unrighteous. Other physical and emotional abuse of those slaves is unrighteous. The list of unrighteous acts could get rather long. Though some considered this to be moral at the time, absolute morality or righteousness will always deem this to be wrong.

We will not be overly concerned with the varieties of capitalism that are outward in form. For instance, we will not be overly comparing liberal market economies with coordinated market economies and so on. This is not primarily a text on economic theory, but the ethics behind economics. We will focus on exploring the benefits of moral-absolute capitalism compared to well-known immoral examples in the market place.

Some may ask what is righteous and what is not? For the sake of argument we will define absolute morality from a Judeo-Christian perspective. Righteousness is then that form of morality which would be so defined by heaven. In such terms then we could say then that there are three shades of capitalism: neutral, righteous and unrighteous. In this book we will examine a number of questions relating to evil and good approaches to capitalism.

Let's challenge ourselves with some questions relating to legality and righteousness. Does the law of the land always define the difference between righteous and unrighteous capitalism? Why do we naively think that if something is legal it must also be absolutely moral, or that if it is illegal it must also be absolutely immoral? Is everything that is legal also righteous? Is everything that is righteous also legal? Is the law of the land always a good guide to what is righteous?

Let's challenge ourselves with some questions about the use of capital. Can capital be used for good and evil? For instance, if clothing is capital, can it be used for good as well as bad? Do we consider clothing, as an object of the weaver's and tailor's art, to be normally morally neutral? Do the means of manufacture via pollution, slavery or some other evil make the clothing then unrighteous? Could the use be unrighteous after manufacture? Even a neutral object like someone's clothing can seem right on the surface and yet be a part of unrighteous capitalism at one point in time or another. Can we always separate the two and is completely guiltless capitalism even possible?

Let's challenge ourselves with some thoughts along the lines of equal opportunity and how it relates to capitalism. What about business opportunities? If business startup laws are just so expensive and complicated that they put the poor at a disadvantage, is that how we create a society of equals? If people are then forced into the black market just to survive whose fault is it? Are illegal immigrants really so evil when they have no way to afford the expensive cost of applying for a work visa or lack the educational or language abilities to navigate a complicated immigration process? Are taxes that molly coddle the wealthy and punish the poor really just and fair?

Let's challenge ourselves with some questions about crime and righteousness. What is really a crime? We normally think of crimes as always unrighteous, but are they? Jesus was murdered by the Roman state in league with its Jewish client political-religious puppets for a so-called crime against the state, being called king of the Jews. Is a crime then always a form of unrighteous capitalism when society's laws are corrupt, when they favor the rich and oppress the poor?

What if a law of the land unrighteously oppresses one group and a so-called crime of helping that group is a righteous act according to the laws of heaven, but a crime in the eyes of human laws? What if all decency and righteousness tells us to give water to a person dying of thirst in the desert southwest just north of the US border with Mexico, but the law of the land makes it a crime punishable by imprisonment, because we will have supposedly aided and abetted an illegal immigrant?

What if the law of the land says that church and state must be separated and those who use the pulpit for political talk break the tax law, but church teachings say that a preacher is also a prophet who must preach against evil, even if that wickedness is political corruption? Of course the state would like to shut the mouths of preachers who stand up against government fraud and corruption. What if it would be illegal to own or preach the Bible as it is in some countries, or to preach certain banned Bible passages as it is in others, simply because it is politically embarrassing to do so? What does a higher law than the law of the land demand?

Now here's a difficult question: Can loyalty to an individual business be at odds with allegiance to one's country, when devotion to country would mean loyalty to the whole market place and not just one small part of it? Let's say that we own a monopoly which creates wealth for itself but to the detriment of the country as a whole. Are we then traitors to country because the very nature of our business hurts national well-being, whether intentional or not?

All businesses are instinctively protective of self. It's a jungle out there. Eventually, a business becomes large enough to harm other businesses. That's the nature of monopolies. Is allowing business to get large enough to hurt other businesses, by its very nature often more unrighteous than righteous? As businesses grow, they can influence the flow of goods in the market for good or evil, such as demanding lower prices from vendors to the hurt of those same vendors. It's not just organized crime that seeks to exclude competitors from the market. Power corrupts does it not?

The Supreme Court recently made a decision to allow greater influence by wealthy corporations, without the balance of such influence by the poor and middle class. Even though corporations are not persons when it comes to voting, they are considered to be persons when it comes to lobbying. The employees of large businesses are not asked their opinions, so such lobbying only represents the muscle power of the chiefs of large corporations. Such an unrighteous decision only exacerbates the already disproportionate influence that the wealthy have in Washington.

Large businesses thus have greater power to lobby for unrighteous laws which protect them and stop competition from smaller businesses and the wider marketplace. If so, do such actions qualify to be called free-market capitalism, when it seems to be protectionist capitalism or crony capitalism? Is this also a form of legal corruption and therefore unrighteous capitalism? Are small time capitalists then sometimes forced to break or bend the law just to survive and feed their families to get around unrighteous laws created at the behest of unrighteous big time capitalists?

Righteous Capitalism

Unrighteous Capitalism

What is unrighteous capitalism? The story of one European city is a metaphor for the dark side of capitalism. Venice is a case study in the results of unrighteous capitalism. Once an affluent, open economy, the rich destroyed it through greed. Venice lost its wealth because the super-wealthy eventually created laws to stop the middle and poor classes from having opportunities to advance in the business world. It was class warfare. The rich made war on the rest and won, but in so doing they destroyed themselves within a hundred years as well.

America was formed to escape the restrictive social classes of Europe, but currently ours are more restrictive than theirs. The poor and middle class cannot afford the educational costs that guarantee top jobs. It costs as much as a house to get a degree from America's top schools. America has dropped to 17th in the world for education. Finland and South Korea top the list of the world's best education.[2] Part of the reason is the value given to educators and ease of access to education.

Some people claim that too many poor people are dependent upon the government for help. Yet, many wealthy have also been dependent upon government for unfair tax breaks and government bailouts. Righteous capitalism does not give us the privilege of hard-heartedness towards the poor.[3] Half of Americans will experience poverty at some time. Declining unions have led to reductions in everyone's wages. Now a quarter of Americans earn poverty-level incomes. People without a high school diploma are 3 to 5 times more likely to be poor than college graduates. Fathers leaving their families make it 3 to 4 times more likely for those families to be poor. Only about a third of disabled people are able to find work. Women experiencing domestic abuse are twice as likely to be unemployed. Women, minorities, children, immigrants, the disabled and female-headed households face far greater poverty rates. Loss of job, declining wages, poor education, fathers leaving, having children and disability are major causes of poverty. The job of a righteous capitalist is to feed the hungry.[4]

Just like in Venice, many of today's wealthy are destroying the system and the freedom that gave them their riches.[5] More and more of us work as poorly paid peasants to greedy corporate oligarchs. National salvation is found in God and the command to love as we shall explore in the second half of this book. Unrighteous capitalism uses business models of self-interest instead of love of God and neighbor.[6]

Simply put, unrighteous capitalism is the evil side of business. Righteous capitalism is the good side. Let's look at some of the results of immoral business practices. We will look at war, coercion, corruption, corporate socialism, state capitalism, greed and extortion. We are all familiar with stories of these things in both business and government.

Unrighteous Capitalism and War

On the dark side of capitalism is war for profit, sacrificing our young men and women for the love of money in battles for market advantage rather than national defense. In a speech delivered in 1933, Major General Smedley Butler, USMC, described some wars as mere unrighteous capitalism in action.

His speech has become reading material for many military leaders over the years. Among other things he said, "Out of war a few people make huge fortunes."[7] At least 21,000 new billionaires and millionaires were created by profits from World War I. Many wars are started to protect private investments at huge cost to the American tax payer. "But the soldier pays the biggest part of the bill."[8]

Under the guise of patriotism, turning blood into gold, war profits for private corporations can amount to anywhere from 20 to 1800 percent above peacetime earnings. To save on war costs, when historically soldiers could have shared in the profits of conquest, we have found that medals are a cheaper reward. Our young people now fight for inexpensive trinkets and pitiful monetary reward.

Rather than allow military might to be used to help business profits abroad, General Butler would "make certain that our military forces are truly forces for defense only."[9] In his 1933 speech Major General Smedley Butler described his military career in not so glowing terms. "I spent most of my time being a high class muscle-man for Big Business, for Wall Street and for the Bankers. In short, I was a racketeer, a gangster for capitalism."[10]

Unrighteous Capitalism and Coercion

The desperate need for money just to survive coerces the weak into doing things that they would not normally want to do. "Markets can often be harsh in compelling people to make unpalatable economic choices any reasonable person would not take under normal conditions"[11] like less pay, illegal immigration, foregoing unaffordable health insurance, cutting food or heat, child labor, prostitution, or moving to cheaper housing.

In wealthy western democracies we believe in the theory of a free market, but in practice do not necessarily experience it for two reasons. 1) A truly free market without regulations would be a Wild West experience with no protections, and 2) too many laws exist to protect the big players from true free-market competition from small businesses. Large corporations often lobby for laws which are pro-business, but not truly pro-market.

A truly free market without any standards of righteousness would be driven primarily by money and "questions of equity and fairness will go unattended and unaddressed"[12] by the powerful. Even with the legal controls that we have in our modern democracies, those who are the least equipped to survive the economic jungle such as the poor suffer the most. Why? There are always ways around the law for those who wish to walk over the bodies of others for profit. Even big businesses which may want to be righteous end up protecting themselves and thereby inadvertently hurting others.

Choices in life are not always as simplistic as choosing between good and evil. Sometimes we must choose between two good alternatives and sometimes the only choices we have are all bad. Economic circumstances force people into hard choices and impossible situations where there may be no good alternative and they can only choose the lesser of two evils.

An example of this is in the story of spies from ancient Israel hiding in the house of Rahab. When officials from the king went looking for them, she had a choice between two evils: lie about where they were or allow them to be arrested and possibly killed. She chose the lesser of two evils and was commended for her faith.[13]

Not all of life's choices are for our benefit. Sometimes we are forced to make a choice between survival and a work situation where our lives are at risk, such as coal miners have faced in the past. The boss may have chosen the dark side of capitalism. Employment is offered by those who are tempted to take high risk opportunities in an insatiable greed for more riches. This creates an immoral winner-take-all ethic where little care is taken for safety and lives that are put at risk or destroyed in the process.

The strong are to bear the burdens of the weak,[14] but that rule is ignored in unrighteous capitalism. "Those who have less of an economic nest egg to begin with and are in need of a more secure safety net are precisely the ones who have to bear the brunt of necessary cost-cutting measures, in contrast to top executives whose compensation packages and 'golden parachutes' are secure."[15]

A completely free-market could only work in a society filled with righteous people who have a moral compass. In a corrupt society we need a regulated market. Laws are (at least they're supposed to be) made to curb the corrupt and are not supposed to be necessary for the righteous. For a corrupt world, "Free market exchange, after all, is concerned merely with creating the highest possible total gains, and not with how such created value is distributed among the transactors, or even whether they are mutually advantageous to all."[16] Who cares if everyone gets a fair deal as long as we make a profit! Right?

When a nation cares little for the poor, those without financial security and without health care, it has failed to live up to the most basic of responsibilities of a civil society. Such "chronic economic distress that is left unattended is an indictment".[17] In this regard, America needs to repent of a grievous sin, yet we excuse our greed and lack of charity by calling such safety nets socialism, which is illogical use of a buzz word.

As we drive our "socialized" roads guided by "socialized" GPS satellites from our "socialized" space program we refuse to help our neighbor as a society because that would be "socialized" medicine or "socialized" welfare? We gladly pay twice as much for corporate "socialized" medicine because we swallow the line that private enterprise is always more efficient than government programs, even though it costs Americans twice as much for health care than any other country on earth and we still don't have everyone covered.

Let's face ourselves honestly: as a nation, we don't really give a damn about the poor. Even when we do try to help, our best efforts often fail. Among the many messages of the Christmas season surely none can create a more joyful experience than to share. Many like to donate extra clothing.[18] *The Volunteer Guide* reports that in America 3.5 million homeless people need clothing, more than a third of them are children. Donating clothing helps the environment by extending their life.

Many charities actually do not follow the spirit of our intentions. Rather than give clothing away, according to *ABC News* many actually resell about 10% of clothes in thrift stores and 90% to clothing manufacturers for recycling. For the righteous capitalist who wants to truly help the poor such practices are great disappointments.[19]

Why is it that after unrighteous capitalists have plundered the poor at home and abroad, destroying jobs and the environment, paying those with jobs lousy wages, with little or no health care, allowing them take the brunt of economic problems, and when they complain, these super-rich dare to call it class warfare? Who has been making war on whom? While the poor and middle class have been experiencing a recession, the super-wealthy around the world have been experiencing an economic boom taking more and more for themselves and leaving the rest of us with less and less.

Unrighteous Capitalism and Legal and Illegal Corruption

Why does the USA have low levels of illegal corruption but is in the middle of the global pack in "legal corruption" like campaign contributions and lobbying?[20] Is a huge key to

US corporate corruption that fact that the CEO is often the board chair and can thus set his own salary almost wherever he wants?[21] Is "cognitive capture" [blinding the thinking] of government by industry's propaganda the result of a great conspiracy, or the natural result of the mistaken belief that an industry's self-interest will also serve the country's interest?[22]

Did Venice create a golden age with free-market capitalism only to end it with elitism and a monopoly by the super-rich? Was this the result of a move towards selfish capitalism that caused Venice to quickly change from the wealthiest city in Europe to a backwater? Is the metaphor of Venice the mistake of its elite class "to conflate its own self-interest with the interests of society as a whole"?

Is it true that elites "don't sabotage the system that created them on purpose"? Was it the natural result of greed that transformed Venice "from a trading power to a museum"?[23] Is America moving in that same direction? If we are not careful, would same result happen here because of our grossly unequal gap between the rich and the poor?

Unrighteous Capitalism: Corporate Socialism or State Capitalism

Some of the most common and most legitimate criticisms of communism were the inefficiency of centralized planning and government theft of private property, but as corporations become larger is that what we have in business, corporate communism? Whether or not it is a state run enterprise or a private one, is it not true that big becomes inefficient? So that leads to some natural questions. Is socialism just state capitalism? Is excessive corporate influence in government just corporate socialism?

When a corporation is small it can only prosper when there is a fair market with a level playing field. When small businesses battle large monopolies (state or private) which control the market place the battle is often almost impossible. Yet, big business monopolies were more than likely one time small businesses that needed a break.

The problem is that as businesses become larger, they become more protective. Big corporations lobby (let's be honest and say bribe) government for protection. It is often done so under the guise of being pro-business. Is there a difference between being pro-market and pro-business? Is the whole market truly served by favoring large businesses that are "too big to fail"? Does government then serve the interests of the few and hurt the interests of the many?

An example of this is Greece in 2012. While much of the problem may be caused by overly generous social spending and lifetime employment guarantees, the corruption of the country's oligarchs cannot be overlooked. "The result, analysts say, is a lack of competition that undermines the economy by allowing the magnates to run cartels and enrich themselves through crony capitalism."[24]

These crony capitalists have created a union-style closed shop at the top, protecting their own interests and hindering fair access to the market. Such lack of competition undermines any economy. Could such unrighteous, crony capitalism be a problem in other countries as well?

In 2012 some say that: "Wall Street is the mother church of capitalism. But its flagship firms are run like Yugoslav workers' collectives"?[25] An East German once told me that Communism was just a perverted form of capitalism, where the party bosses made capital of the rest. Could it be that 20th century Communism was similar to 21st century capitalism? The communist oligarchy was the communist party, with the provincial head of a party organization earning 25 times more than average, much like a CEO in the west? [26] Could it be then that 21st century global capitalism is not that much different?

Is China an example of state capitalism? Is the system in many ways similar to western crony capitalism where being close to the state is "how the system really works"? Is it as the book *Red Capitalism* claims that, "China is a family-run business"?[27] If so, is it also true that "China's plutocrats don't fight the state because they are the state"?[28]

When it comes to the super rich, 42% live in America, followed by China, Germany, Switzerland and Japan?[29] How much do the super-rich in America, Germany, Switzerland and Japan influence the affairs of state for their own benefit as opposed to the benefit of the whole market?

Is the example in socialist China just another form of what happens in the west where big businesses lobby selfishly against some necessary actions which may hurt their businesses a little but in reality could help the broader economy greatly? Is being pro-business always the same as being pro-market? Do big businesses often lobby against being pro-market as they become self-protective? Is it true that real capitalism lacks a strong lobby because most lobbying in America is for protection of big businesses and to restrict competition from smaller players? Is the excessive influence of big business in our legislatures then actually the opposite of true free market capitalism?[30] Is it a form of corporate socialism? I think so.

When large corporations receive government subsidies and tax breaks not available to the rest of us do we have corporate socialism? When large corporations are run like socialist states within a state for the benefit of the executive apparatchik, do we have corporate socialism? When health care is provided by the big corporation at twice the price that a government system would cost, do we have corporate socialism? I think so.

America has been called the land of "boring work environments, go-nowhere jobs".[31] When corporations provide health care and states engage in the marketplace, what do we have? When does capitalism begin and socialism end? The words are so misused in public conversation that we fail to understand which

34

is which. Does the conversation disguise the fact that corrupt, unrighteous capitalism can be engaged in by private as well as government entities? Is the real question not who is the capitalist, but whether or not that person or entity is engaging in righteous capitalism that benefits society as a whole or unrighteous capitalism that benefits just an elite few?

What is the real difference between the greedy American CEO and the Chinese Communist party plutocrat? Have not both used any federal influence they can muster for self-benefit rather than for the benefit of society as a whole? Have not both taken the large share of the pie for selfish gain at the expense of ordinary workers? Is there any difference other than how they play the game in their cultural context? Has not each been playing the same game of unrighteous capitalism driven by greed?

Unrighteous Capitalism and Greed

Could we say that a challenge to every economy is how to have capitalism create wealth for all without capitalists creating wealth for just the few?[32] Could it be that our central economic ill is what some call rent-seeking, unproductive wealthy people living off of investments that add no value to civilization compared with those capitalists who are genuinely providing innovative improvements to society?[33] Could a once innovative company which provided great benefits to all slowly evolve into a rent-seeking monster that later prevents a market from being truly free?

Greed and Capitalism

Business too often becomes war instead of mutual cooperation for mutual benefit of all parties involved, customers, employees and society at large. War only destroys. It does not build. When we are never satisfied we fight and when corporations fight both sides lose.

We take people to court and the only ones who win in court are the lawyers. We take on too much debt and the only winners there are the banks. We become proud and everyone loses. We become vengeful and destroy others. In short, we forget the ideals of our youth and slowly slide into a game of corporate warfare that benefits only winners and hurts losers.

Greed is bad for capitalism because the resulting fights between businesses, inside corporations and even among family members only destroy and do not build wealth and peace for all.[34]

Greed and Pride

The evil side of capitalism includes people who seem to believe that they are righteous in their own eyes. Yet here they are described as being filled with pride while they hunt the poor like game to be killed, even boasting of their heart's desires and praising others who are just as greedy.[35]

In Augustine's commentary on Psalm 10, he described God's great anger with such greedy capitalists who engage in "fraud and wickedness" placing them in the same class as Antichrist.[36]

Greed and Plunder

Evil capitalists do not necessarily engage in murder directly, but the result of their actions is the same. While they plunder the lives and fortunes of others they are actually destroying their own souls. Their end effect of their own greed robs them of life.[37]

What profit is it if a man gains the whole world but loses his life, his soul?

Greed and Loneliness

"A selfish man cares for nobody; there is none to take care of but himself, yet he will scarcely allow necessary rest to himself, and the people he employs."[38] He or she is never satisfied with enough. In pursuit of the world, they tread on friends and family until they are alone.

Even the so-called friends that greedy people accumulate, they are never sure of, whether or not they are true friends or merely fair weather friends only interested in their money. Woe to the rich man who loses everything, because even these bought friends will vanish. Greed causes a lonely and empty life.[39] If a person has nothing financially, but a few friends, then that person is very rich indeed, because money can't buy true friends.

Greed and Family Destruction

A greedy man troubles his own household, "he is a torment to himself and his family by his avariciousness and penury, and a curse to those with whom he deals."[40] Favoritism and greed over inheritance drives family members apart.

Greed in business creates workaholics who neglect their families. Divorce and separation from family members is the price paid. But, those who hate this perverted kind of capitalism with its bribes and neglect of family will live.[41]

Greed and Character

Greed makes people weak in character. They get rich via unethical means, taking advantage of fragile people by either paying low wages or providing pitiful health care and other benefits.

Money causes people to fall prey to the trap of bribery and ill-gotten gains. The deception of dishonest riches makes people think they will be happy, but in reality it makes them miserable and destroys their lives.[42]

Greed and Leadership

A leader who uses judgment rather than destructive greed and bribery brings stability.[43] Greedy corporate and government leaders can never get enough. "They regard neither God's glory, nor the peoples good, but only the satisfaction of their own base desires."[44]

Avaricious people are impudent, greedy dogs and ignorant shepherds of people, unaware of the destruction they bring on themselves and those they manage.[45]

Greedy Eyes, Greedy Hearts

What we look for and what our hearts desire have consequences. When our eyes and hearts are fixed on covetousness, then manslaughter and oppression and extortion are not far behind. The lust for dishonest gain leads to the shedding of innocent blood either directly or indirectly.

Greedy individuals are tempted to oppress weaker employees, clients or competitors by not paying a decent wage, overcharging for services and trying to shut down other market players. Avaricious people are tempted to extort money or business deals from others.[46]

Greed and Flattery

A boss who praises you, but pays terribly may be giving all that he or she can. The market demands that we all must accept the wages that a business can afford. But, the sweet talk of greedy people is not to be trusted. And, the praises of a CEO sound hollow if he or she takes home more before lunch on the first day of work than the average worker makes all year.

Flattery is hollow and meaningless without actions to back it up. Some corporate leaders speak of love and fuzzy feelings of teamwork, but are in reality greedy for unjust gain.[47] The gold watch after decades of loyal service is a hollow reward if the boss has taken a grossly selfish portion of the profits.

Greed and Guise

We all put on a disguise to some extent, but greedy people may be among the most adept at it. They may look good on the outside but it's just an act. Unrighteous capitalism is disguised as doing good.

The vile and selfish trading practices of monopolies masquerade as a free-market but are in fact corporate protectionism, crony capitalism. The façade fools simple people, but thinkers can see that within they are full of greedy corruption.[48]

Greed and Short-sightedness

Greed is a short-sighted approach to life. Businesses that take short-cuts eventually lose community trust and those companies do not last. Avarice destroys an industry's long term prospects.

Honesty is for the long haul, for businesses that want to last.

The saying, "he who dies with the most toys wins" is for losers who define human life by material things. Possessions do not define our lives. Real wealth is defined by those things which last an eternity.[49]

Greed and other Evils

Greed is among a list of society's worst evils. It accompanies adultery, murder, theft, deceit,[50] maliciousness,[51] extortion,[52] lasciviousness,[53] immorality,[54] quarreling and dishonest gain.[55] Greed is one of the great evils of our age.

Because of greed, unrighteous capitalism destroys both society and the individuals involved. Unrighteous capitalism is not long-term capitalism, but short-sighted capitalism that ignores the damaging consequences of corruption.

Unrighteous Capitalism and Extortion

When the organized crime squeezes money out of legitimate businesses, they can go to jail. But, when large corporations crush small business with excessive fees or unaffordable discounts, governments do little or nothing. Extortion is normal business practice in a corrupt market place. Ancient Roman soldiers were known for it[56] and only the manner of corruption has changed since. When companies overcharge customers there is little or no difference.

Another form of extortion results from monopolies. Not all monopolies are wrong. God has a monopoly on everything, but it is not an oppressive monopoly. Government, by its nature is a monopoly. The problem is not the fact of monopoly but the corruption that too often accompanies monopoly.

In the hands of mere human beings, even righteous individuals, oppression goes along with power and money. Why do we think that religious Europe and New England were such oppressive places? Even the most righteous of us is blind to our own sins, our use of oppression and extortion. We need to be careful to avoid them.

We are taught to charge "what the market will bear" rather than do what is right. Yet, there is a difference for the righteous capitalist. There are many forms of unrighteous capitalism. What principles make for righteous capitalism? Let's look at that in the second half of the book.

Unrighteous Capitalism Destroys

Any business or nation that is built by bloodshed, violent injustice and bribery is building in its own destruction. Shoe merchants, copper miners, explosives manufacturers, steel companies and tool makers all tend to love war, because then they can make huge profits selling to the government. But our young men and women on the front lines pay the price. They pay with their lives and they pay with destroyed emotions and their families pay dearly as well. If we have to go to war, let's make sure that it is really necessary and for self-defense rather than motivated by profit.

But, bloodshed is not just on the battlefields. Blood is figuratively-speaking in the streets of our nations as our markets engage in commercial warfare. Indirectly, many businesses cause blood to be shed either by selling cancer-causing products like cigarettes or by paying such low wages that people are forced to resort to self-destructive means of making a living, like selling drugs or turning to prostitution.

Violent injustice is in our prisons which are filled overwhelmingly with the poor. Although some white collar crime is punished, most of our prisons are filled with criminals charged with far less costly crimes.

Bribery is rampant in our culture. A comedian once suggested that perhaps we should insist that our politicians dress like race car drivers, wearing the logos of those who contributed to their campaigns and whose lobbying they listen to.

Poor people find it almost impossible to get an audience with legislators, but the wealthy can much more easily. They own Washington and Berlin and Canberra and the poor have no voice except to strike. Striking is a destructive plea for help, when no other means seems to avail. When the poor cry in pain, few hear their voices, and the wealthy often ignore them, but when the rich are challenged their cry is heard everywhere.

The ancient prophet Micah's warned that a nation or business built by destroying lives, by bribery and injustice will be plowed as a field.[57]

Righteous Capitalism

The *Caux Round Table* (Moral Capitalism at Work) is a good resource for a moral point of view.[58] The *Caux Round Table's Pegasus Monthly Newsletter* is an excellent resource. In this book I argue for a higher standard than fickle human morality, an absolute morality from a greater source. I reason from a viewpoint of the theology behind morality and how it might apply to righteous capitalism.

To what level of unrighteous capitalism has America sunk? Do we need to rescue America from the clutches of today's robber barons and return it to the democracy of Thomas Jefferson, a vision of egalitarian capitalism without the cronies?[59] Even Bill Gates, whose company was sometimes accused of trying to monopolize an industry, said that capitalism must do good things.[60] Some believe that the left hates the rich, but is that the truth? Is it not that they hate the predators, unjustified privilege, unfairness and crony capitalism?[61]

If Winslow Jones pioneered the hedge fund, George Doriot prepared modern venture capitalism, and Victor Prosner initiated hostile takeovers, now disguised under the name "private equity," could these three be described as the fathers of the instability of modern financial capitalism, of today's unrighteous capitalism? Are these three systems among the main drivers of today's super-rich as some believe?[62] Is this really what we could call a form of capitalism that benefits the country as a whole?

What is righteous capitalism? Is it not the using of goods and services for the improvement of the whole of society, not just a single company or individual?

The Great Principle of Righteous Capitalism

The greatest commandment of righteous capitalism is an antique one:

> *Thou shalt love the Lord thy God with all thy heart, and with all thy soul, and with all thy mind... Thou shalt love thy neighbour as thyself.*[63]

The second half of that commandment is called the *Golden Rule* and it is a principle found in every major religion since ancient Babylon and the *Code of Hammurabi*. The *Lex talionis* (an eye for an eye) is a principle of reciprocity (fairness). May I suggest that the *Golden Rule* also applies to business and is therefore a standard of righteous capitalism? That great principle essentially includes the love of God.

48

We cannot claim to love God unless we treat God in our neighbors with love.[64]

May I suggest that the so called "gold rule" is the standard of unrighteous capitalism? The one who has the gold rules, or as some like it, the one with the gold makes the rules. Unrighteous capitalism is essentially selfish.

Does not selfish capitalism ask, "Am I my brother's keeper?"[65] Does not unselfish capitalism answer, "Love your neighbor as yourself"?[66]

The Greatest Commandment must be the most important principle in sustainable and honorable capitalism, love God and neighbor.[67] How does this work in business? Let's look at some examples.

Righteous Capitalism and Giving

Solomon advised the wealthy to give generously. Wealth given away may seem to be lost, like casting bread upon water. But there is a universal principle involved here. That bread seemingly cast away will return even though it may seem to be lost forever. Our goal ought to be to spread material blessings around to as many people as possible. We never know! This could be the day we die and what better day to die than a day when we gave selflessly.

We easily excuse our actions, saying we don't have time or don't trust that the money will be well-used. But what better use of our money could there be than giving freely? Wealth deceives us that it is profit for us, but money is no real profit unless it is given away. Philanthropy is where the real profit lies.

Our real job on earth is not creating profits for our companies and ourselves, but to be a blessing to others. We have good work to do. Take a lesson from the rain cloud. It is no good unless it empties itself. Let's not be tired of giving, because in God's time, we will reap abundantly.[68]

Giving and the Causes of Poverty

One of the first topics of conversation, when speaking of giving, is the sweeping false accusation often leveled against the poor of laziness. It is a lie foisted upon us by those who wish to find an excuse not to give. There are many causes of poverty and slothfulness is one of the least.

Even if laziness were the main cause of poverty, which it is not, God does not give us the privilege of hard-heartedness towards the poor.[69] Half of Americans will experience poverty at some time in their lives. Declining unions have led to reductions in everyone's wages. Now, in the early part of the 21st century, a quarter of Americans earn poverty-level incomes.

People without a high school diploma are 3 to 5 times more likely to be poor than college graduates. Fathers leaving their families make it 3 to 4 times more likely for those same families to be poor. Only about a third of disabled people are able to find work. Women experiencing domestic abuse are twice as likely to be unemployed.

Women, minorities, children, immigrants, the disabled and female-headed households face far greater poverty rates than the rest of us. Loss of job, declining wages, poor education, fathers leaving, having children and disability are major causes of poverty. Slothfulness is a cause in only a small minority of cases. Our job is to feed the hungry.[70]

Poverty may also be caused by overpopulation, inadequate distribution methods, rising costs, inadequate education, unemployment and under-employment, crime and unjust incarceration, environmental degradation, foolish financial decisions, excessive medical expenses, sickness, mergers and acquisitions, hostile takeovers, greed, the cost and devastation of war, natural disasters, industrial changes, recessions, discrimination, pregnancy out of wedlock, immigrant status, gang presence and a host of other things.

Laziness is also a motive for those who seek quick riches such as robbery, drug smuggling, scams, usurious interest rates and similar legal or illegal get-rich-quick schemes. Righteous capitalists understand that honest work not lazy covetousness is the way to true success. They do not engage in legal or illegal swindles. They also consider the poor who most often suffer not because of laziness but causes like those mentioned above, and they are extravagant in their giving.[71]

Giving and Wealth Addiction

A popular message implies that it is easy for a rich Christian to enter heaven. Jesus said just the opposite.[72] False teachings imply that wealth is always God's blessing and poverty his curse, but that ignores wealth gotten by dishonest means and poverty through no fault of the poor. Was Jesus a sinner because he died on the cross? Such thinking is illogical but popular.

It has been said that it is hard for a wealthy person to enter heaven? Why is it such a battle? "The wealthy are generally held captive by their wealth."[73] Whether we are rich or poor we may be blessed or not. The blessings of heaven are independent of our financial status here on earth. The greatest blessings of all are spiritual. It is impossible for rich or poor to enter heaven, except for the greatest miracle of all time, divine grace: "where humanity is helpless, God can."[74]

Who is the most popular Christian outside of the Bible? We may think of famous theologians or reformers but the most popular is Nicholas of Myra, who was loved by many in his time and those who read his story today. The fiction surrounding him has grown to the point that he is the second most important Christmas character after Jesus.

Why is he so popular? He read the story where Jesus suggested that one rich young man sell everything giving the money to the poor.[75] Though he was very wealthy, Nicholas spent his life giving it away and touched the lives of thousands. He saved many from financial ruin, helped out in disasters, defended people in court from false charges, provided food during famines, saved children from slavery, travelers from murder and prayed and saved sailors from shipwreck. The real Saint Nicholas is loved because he made crooked roads straight and rough ways smooth.[76] Shall we?

Wealth can become an addiction just like alcoholism. If a person cannot handle the responsibility, then perhaps giving it up altogether is the only viable alternative. Perhaps it is the final step on the road to perfection. After all Jesus' words were that the rich young man only lacked one thing and what better legacy could there be than giving it all away.

What would be our society's greatest addictions? When we speak of addiction, we may think of alcohol or drugs, but those are not our world's greatest addictions. Our economy relies upon creating addictions to sell products. Could it be that two of our greatest addictions are unhealthy foods and materialism?

Advertising deceives us that material goods make an abundant life and politics deceives us that our salvation begins with a materialistic solution to our nation's woes. We are constantly fed the lie that materialism and degenerate foods will create the abundant life. Yet, almost every wise sage in history has warned against greedy materialism because that is not life.[77] There is a way that we might have truly rich and satisfying lives, but most people will ignore it.[78] Crafting righteous capitalism, the only kind that produces a full life, begins in the sheepfold of a house of faith.

Giving to Employees

Who is your role model? Is it the Good Shepherd or a hired hand?[79] All church pastors read the words which challenge them about false leaders and say to themselves, "I hope that is not me." Yet all leaders, managers, CEO's, generals, politicians, all except the one, are mere hirelings. We must face the fact that we are being described here and seek to become real leaders. And what is real leadership? The cross tells us what real leadership is, self-sacrifice.

Even Jesus' disciples ran away during difficult times. Business owners often compare themselves by how big their companies are, how long they have been in business, how many dollars they have made or other such egotistical measures. But, success as a leader is not measured by such silly standards but by standing firm when the wolf attacks. A great corporate shepherd is one willing to die for his or her people.

A great business leader is that person that is first of all a great shepherd of the company, willing to die for the employees. That means that the company CEO or the small business owner is the first to take a pay cut, the first to stand up for the jobs and the pay rates given to the employees, before the union can, before the first whimper of complaint from the line can be heard.

Of course, that also must be balanced. Overly generous companies cannot survive competition. Greed also applies to unions that are sometimes willing destroy companies for a pay raise. They can kill the goose that lays the golden egg. However, before CEO's complain about union wages, they must first look at what they take out of the company in salary and benefits. Is it is grossly gluttonous or just and fair?

Giving is the Job Description of the Rich

Paul the Apostle had a word of advice for the rich. It is simple but profound. Don't be proud or full of yourself.[80]

That is a hard job when people are flattering you all day long. It is hard for Hollywood celebrities. It is hard for bosses surrounded by the fawning flattery of those dependent upon them for their pay checks. Saint Paul also said not to trust in riches. Riches can be here today, gone tomorrow. Wall Street can crash overnight. Real estate bubbles can burst leaving us with larger debts than property is worth.

Fortunes can be lost in war as hostile armies destroy everything that has been built over a lifetime. Just ask anyone who lived in Europe during World War II.

I once met a woman whose family had to just walk away from everything they owned in the German colonies of Eastern Europe. The family farm was lost forever. They marched west with nothing but the clothes on their backs and their daughter was born on the side of the road as they made their journey to safety in the west.

Paul then charged the wealthy to be rich in good works, ever ready to distribute help and extravagantly generous.[81]

If it is more blessed to give than to get[82] then surely the wealthy have the opportunity, indeed the responsibility to experience one of the greatest blessings that life has to offer, the opportunity to give so much to so many.

Righteous Capitalism and Lending

The poor are often the ones who are unable to negotiate the most favorable finance rates. It is also the poor who pay the highest credit card interest rates, perhaps as high as 30 or 40 percent. The rich are either able to negotiate lower interest because of the size of their accounts, have fees waived or in most cases pay no interest at all because they are able to pay their bills off before interest accrues.

The poor are the ones who fall into desperate situations like needing to pay bills or feed their families, and are tempted to foolishly put such necessities on a credit card. Some of them owe so much and pay such high interest rates that will be slaves to their debt for a very long time. Although banks may claim to treat all customers alike, that is not true. People with very large accounts get very special treatment.

Lending to the Poor

Biblical capitalism has a lot to say about charging interest to the poor. It specifically forbids it, turning upside down what many in the banking industry assume to be perfectly okay, profiting from the suffering of others at extortion racket rates.[83]

58

A righteous capitalist seeks to put no such burden on the destitute who are borrowing not for luxury or business but for necessity.

Lending for Relief instead of Usury

Poverty is great misery and heartache and unfortunately all too common. Humanity has never been able to solve the problem of the penniless. However, the righteous capitalist recognizes the responsibility to relieve those who have fallen on hard times.

Righteous lending is engaged in by those who have compassion towards the needy.[84] They want to serve their impoverished neighbors and do something good for them within their ability.[85] The ones who are able are the super wealthy.

For the rest of us, there is an important limitation because in a world where stockholders scream for dividends and growth and CEO's pressure employees to generate income, one person's lonely voice calling for a higher standard of business ethics may fall on deaf ears.

We are only responsible for what we can do and sadly that may be very little in a culture that puts profit before pity. The ones who can help the most are the very elite. Instead of hoarding their real job ought to be sharing.

Lending to Fellow Citizens

An interesting law in the ancient world required the occasional loan between citizens to be interest free, but not so with foreigners.[86] We could speculate that the difference was that those foreigners would have normally been involved in trade as opposed to agriculture and therefore it would have been a higher risk loan.

How this would play out today where situations are far more complicated would be a matter of some discussion.

We may however, be shocked to find that even a one percent interest charge was scandalous in the days of Nehemiah.[87]

Righteous Lending Criteria

In strictly private loans between citizens righteous people generously lend as able. Can this also apply to the banking world? It is not as easy as it sounds, because loan officers who wish to be righteous capitalists work with many constraints. However, it is possible.

Loans in the banking world are gauged upon several criteria such as capacity, capital, collateral, conditions and character.[88] Another measure is also considered by the compassionate capitalist, need.[89] If there is any possible way to help those who really need a loan at a favorable rate, a compassionate lender will search for it without at the same time betraying an employer's trust.

Lending Usury in Heaven's Eyes

We may think that all this discussion of usury is naïve today. We live in a world that expects it and have little to no experience of societies that avoid charging interest. A brief examination of Islamic interest-free banking reveals a system with some interesting lessons in this regard.

Christians and Jews may be interested to know that God seems to be of the opinion that charging interest is an abomination.[90] Hence, it is something that the righteous capitalist will contemplate with a sense of importance.

The Highest Standard of Lending

Anyone who has read even the slightest amount of Jesus' teachings may notice that he reached for even higher standards than the letter of the law. He often reiterated a common theme of his life, heaven's standard of self-sacrificial giving. He taught that in our private lives we are to lend to those who cannot possibly repay.[91] This implies the forgiveness of debt, a call that banks can make in the case of uncollectible debts.

Righteous capitalists will seek to balance their responsibilities to keep their lending institutions afloat and yet show the mercy demanded of a higher institution, heaven. In their private lives, righteous capitalists are generous to a fault.

Righteous Capitalism frees Slaves

In politics, slavery is a dirty word, but slavery still exists under different names. Certainly all would agree that the kind of slavery that existed in America's southern plantations was a gross evil, the result of kidnapping. Also sex slavery today is a heinous crime.

However, anciently there were several other kinds of slave, which are tolerated today under different names. War reparations, prison chain gangs and the slavery of debt are still forms of slavery today. Just as the rich rule over the poor, so is the debtor a slave to the moneylender.[92]

In ancient Israel, economic slaves were to be freed after six years of service.[93] There was to be no such thing as long term debt. The morally superior social law of that nation was designed to relieve and restore the suffering. *Relief* and *restoration* are two important principles that every righteous capitalist will want to think about in philanthropy.

Our morally inferior banking system allows for long term debt and its associated financial slavery. Ancient systems were sometimes more righteous, more civilized than ours. "Limiting debt slavery to a maximum period of six years of service was in effect a de facto cap on the amount of the loan that the lender might retrieve from the borrower through the latter's indentured service."[94]

What an incredible system! "Debt, rather than war, was the principal cause of bondage in Israel... Debtors and their families were sold into slavery to cover arrears or in the aftermath of a debt default. However, there was a maximum term of six years of service after which debt slaves were to be given back their freedom, and all outstanding obligations were wiped clean."[95]

Unrighteous capitalists in the modern market happily subjugate naïve people to long term debt for profit and seem to show little or no remorse. They build master-servant relationships whereby their indebted victims provide them a continuous stream of income. They are modern feudal lords earning tribute from oppressed serfs.

Righteous capitalists will find the model that ancient Israel was given for liberation from debt fascinating. The wonderful debt forgiveness of the sabbatical year was intended to be a rest from heavy financial burdens.

It was the Sabbath principle applied to finance and was designed to be a chance for a restoration which the debtor could not normally attain without help. It was designed to restore lost equality in a nation of equals. The righteous capitalist who may possibly restore those enslaved to debt in the spirit of this ancient law, has a wonderful opportunity.

Righteous Capitalism and Wisdom

There is something more profitable than financial gain. It is wisdom. No collection of jewels or houses or expensive cars or private jets or yachts can be compared to the true wealth of genuine wisdom. Righteous capitalists value wisdom highly. They consider wisdom to be a core value in business.

The Bible is one of the world's greatest sources of wisdom. It is the greatest text book of righteous capitalism.[96] Wisdom is worth more than any amount of money and insight is far more valuable than a great income.[97]

Righteous Capitalism and Money

One of the great problems of money is that we learn to trust it, even though it deceives us. It deceives us into thinking that we are superior to others, that we are invincible and that we can control the direction of our lives. In reality, none of us can truly control outside forces and none of us is worth more than a mixture of a few common chemicals.

Yet, on the other hand, every human life is priceless, even those that we tend to look down upon. Those who trust in money will fail, because money is an undependable and misleading friend. On the other hand, righteous capitalists are honorable people and will flourish like green leaves in spring.[98] How does a righteous capitalist relate to money?

Righteous Capitalism free of Bribes

Many modern business practices are no better than murder. What else do we call chemical pollution, foods that cause cancer and wars of aggression created by international business interests? Those who profit from such schemes are no better than those who bribe judges or plant false evidence to allow a murderer to escape the death penalty or life in prison.[99]

One of the great problems in inherited positions is that the righteousness of former generations may be tossed aside and bribery and corruption become the order of the day.[100] The heirs may not follow the moral ideals of their forebears. That is one reason why the German monarchy was an elected position rather than an inherited one. That is also why wise corporate heads bring in leadership from outside of the founding family. Choosing someone with ability is wiser than favoritism.

Ten Marks of a Righteous Capitalist

Psalm 15 describes ten hallmarks of a righteous person and it interesting to contemplate in light of this discussion of a righteous capitalist. Let's ask the question, who is allowed to do business in God's economy? Who will trade in his holy marketplace?

1) Righteous capitalists walk uprightly, blameless and operating businesses with integrity.

2) Righteous capitalists do what is right. They do not overcharge or undercut or misrepresent merchandise. They do not engage in fraudulent business practices such as operating scales that show false weights to customers.[101]

3) Righteous capitalists speak the truth in their hearts. They are sincere and truthful. If we think about the truth it will be revealed in what we do.

4) Righteous capitalists do not initiate slander or malicious gossip about competitors or coworkers.

5) Righteous capitalists do no evil towards a neighbor.

6) Righteous capitalists do not take up and wallow in the slander or malicious gossip begun by others.

7) Righteous capitalists despise the practices of evil capitalists and honor those who are straight in business. To whom do we show honor, honest business people or super-wealthy ones without asking how honest they are?

8) Righteous capitalists keep their promises, even when it hurts. They know that honor is more important than the money lost.

9) Righteous capitalists lend money to the poor interest free putting their protection ahead of profit.

10) Righteous capitalists refuse to take bribes to give false testimony. For instance, they will refuse to lie in court about products which exploit or harm the poor.

What is the result of such integrity of the righteous capitalist? The Psalm was a song to be sung about upright people who will never be moved. Business conditions may come and go, but the righteous capitalist will survive after all the unrighteous ones are long gone.

Righteous Capitalism is Honest Money

A righteous person's actions generally lead towards a good life. Though calamities happen to us all and unplanned catastrophes can cause great pain, honest living provides a greater percentage of real success in life. However, those who lead dishonest lives are punished by the results of such a life, with or without any legal intervention.[102]

Empty get-rich-quick schemes are not the way to true success. People who engage in deceptive advertising and similar dishonest business practices are actually abject failures ethically. There is no substitute for work. It is the slow but honest way to financial success.[103]

To dishonest corporations and unrighteous capitalists that have looted nations, God has a warning. They shall loot you. The violence of unrighteous capitalists who con their countries into going to war to protect business interests shall not go unpunished. Those who build their homes by unjust gain will suffer. They shame their own households. They reap woes to themselves.[104]

Unrighteous capitalists use feigned words, fabricated stories, and clever lies to sell products. They make merchandise of us. Their condemnation has been hanging over them like a pall for a long time.[105]

Unrighteous capitalists have gone the way of Cain, who killed his own brother for personal gain. They run greedily after the way of Balaam, who took bribes to deceive people with counterfeit religion. Like Korah, they will be destroyed in their own rebellion against the rules of righteous business practices.[106]

Money is worthless on Judgment day

The righteous capitalist knows that a judgment day is coming and wants to stand on that day with a good track record. Money won't bribe the Lord on that day. It will be so worthless that people will throw their silver and gold into the streets.[107]

Righteous Capitalism more than Money

Luke 12 contains a commentary on righteous capitalism. An honest entrepreneur is always on guard against the hypocrisy of those who trample on their fellow human beings. He is not fooled by those who claim to keep secret business deals which hurt others and knows that even the most private of business meetings will someday be made very public. It will be shouted from the housetops. Going down the road with dishonest business people is a foolish trap set by those who desire quick profits, but the honest capitalist is not afraid of them. He or she fears only God.

The good business person knows the hypocrisy of the commercial world, but trusts in God's providence, and is satisfied to rely on him rather than making avaricious plans. As God provides for all of us, the righteous capitalist joins God in that heavenly enterprise of providing for fellow human beings, just as God provides for the smallest sparrow. When asked why he will not engage in corruption, he is not ashamed to confess God before others.

When asked why they will not engage in corruption righteous capitalists confess Christ. They know that a person's life does not consist in an abundance of material things. And on that great day, Christ will be glad to confess him before the angels of God.

Those who live lives of persistent hostility against God are in danger of having blasphemed against the Holy Spirit, a sin which will never be forgiven, because they will never repent of it.

Covetousness is not in the righteous entrepreneur's tool box. He or she has seen many a friend get greedy only to die in misery after accumulating a wealth of material possessions for nothing. This is the danger faced even by an upright business person who may have accumulated money as a reward for honest work. The money is not the purpose of it all. Instead of thanking God for the opportunity to share with others, a greedy person's life is soon over and none of us can take it with us. Money is a tool to be used for good, not selfishness.

Another temptation in the world of capitalism is worry over money and status. The righteous capitalist has a great secret that the unrighteous capitalist is largely ignorant of. He does not worry as much. The unrighteous capitalist creates enemies, engages in shady activities and must worry about being caught by the law. Unrighteous capitalists worry about status. The righteous capitalist is humble, could care less about such vanities and knows that God will always provide the most important necessities of life.

The righteous capitalist is not interested in accumulating expensive but worthless trinkets and other overpriced assets that help nobody. His goal in life is not selfish accumulation but giving. He gladly spends his life selling what he has to give it all away.

Nicholas was born of wealthy Christian parents in what is today southern Turkey. It was a Greek area at the time. He followed Jesus' comments to a wealthy young man[108] to sell his possessions and give the money to the poor. Nicholas spent the bulk of his life doing just that and is known for his generosity to those in need.

One story tells of his providing a dowry for three daughters who, without it, were bound for a life of sexual slavery. Little bags of coins were tossed in a window landing in stockings and a shoe, giving rise to several Christmas traditions. As we think of making crooked roads straight and rough ways smooth in preparation for Christ's coming,[109] it is good to follow a wonderful example of giving like that of Saint Nicholas.

They may trip off to Paris for a few days' shopping in their personal jet and everyone seems to go "Ooooh!" In reality they are fools who care not for others and deserve no adulation. The righteous capitalist is not impressed. Though they are chauffeured around in a million dollar limousine with a diamond encrusted steering wheel, they are clowns and God is not impressed. The righteous capitalist does not waste time on such stupid toys. There are more important things to spend money on, like a world in need of help.

Where our money, is that is also where our hearts are. If our money is spent on costly thingamajigs that will melt when the earth disappears, then our hearts are hollow and empty. If our money is spent on making the lives of others better, then our hearts are in the right place and we belong to that most exclusive club of all, the righteous capitalists.

The righteous capitalist will be found doing good things with money when Christ returns and not wasting it on the frivolity that infects so many of the rich. None of us know the timing of the second coming, but the righteous capitalist is always ready. While the unrighteous capitalist continues to beat up on others, taking advantage of them for profit, the righteous capitalist knows that evil will not prevail in the judgment day.[110]

Righteous Capitalism and Pricing

Today's common practice is pricing according to "what the market will bear." It goes along with pricing according to demand. The ancient church father *Thomas Aquinas* taught that "raising prices in response to high demand was a type of theft."[111] In other words an unjust price is a type of fraud. Any unfair earnings made in trade are immoral gain made by not actually creating something. Such dealings break the Golden Rule.

The righteous capitalist does not raise prices of building materials after a natural disaster. Righteous capitalists charge prices based on the cost of materials and labor and do not capitalize on the desperation of the buyer. In this way the righteous capitalist contributes to a moral economy, where pricing is just and fair and good. This honest approach to business and government leads to a proper balance between social needs and economic freedom.

Righteous Capitalism no Love of Money

The righteous capitalist recognizes that the love of money is a sucker trap and avoids it. He knows that it is an addiction that can never be satisfied with enough. The righteous capitalist is not hypnotized by useless expensive items that add no value to life.[112]

The good entrepreneur has seen how the love of money has caused all kinds of evil and even ruined lives. There are plenty of examples of it in the market place. The good business person is wise and sees the danger and avoids the love of money.[113]

The righteous capitalist knows that when people are lovers of money times will be more difficult. In fact the love of money makes a society dangerous, terrible, because of the atrocities that people will commit. A society that loves money is one filled with murder, theft and destruction of people's lives, much like the modern world. The righteous capitalist sees this peril and avoids the love of money.[114]

Advertising is often designed to make us dissatisfied, to entice a lust for more, to create covetous desires. Contentment is a trait of the righteous capitalist. They are not obsessed with getting more material things. They are satisfied with what they have.[115]

Righteous Capitalism and Tithing

Tithing is a principle of proportional giving from the Hebrew Scriptures. God has given us everything that we have. Every breath we take and every beat of our hearts come from him. He expects our generosity in return or if you care. God expects that we be generous because he is. In ancient Israel, three tenths of a person's income was budgeted at different times and for different reasons.

One tenth was given to God's work and in turn God promised to pour out blessings upon the giver.[116] Those who did not give were described as thieves and those who did give were promised material abundance. Another tenth was given to the poor in the third and sixth year of a seven year cycle.[117] Another tenth was to be saved and consumed at the annual worship festivals,[118] in some ways similar to a vacation savings plan.

Though under the New Covenant Christians no longer see themselves as being under the letter of the law, nevertheless the principles of that law remain as guides to righteous capitalism. Giving may not always be an exact tenth but will be proportional and based upon what is in a person's heart. Whereas a miserly or cash-strapped giver may give either a tenth or find reasons for giving less, a generous heart might find ways to give even more than the bare minimum.

Examples of capitalists tithing that are well-known are William Colgate of Colgate-Palmolive, James Kraft of Kraft Foods and Henry Heinz of Heinz Ketchup. Such successful capitalists made God a partner in their businesses and began giving God a tenth and were materially blessed for it.[119]

The tithe given to God had a higher priority than the tithe given to the poor. We might think that is wrong, but perhaps we need to see it from heaven's perspective. The tithe given to the church is primarily for the Gospel, the announcement of permanent good news.

The poor are a high priority to the righteous capitalist, but their eternal salvation is more important than their temporary salvation from the suffering of this world. Jesus' own words regarding being anointed with expensive oil which could have been sold and the money given to the poor, show that he thought the work of God has a higher priority over even the needs of the poor.[120]

The case of the widow's mite is extraordinary. There was a widow who was among a group of people being mistreated by political and religious leaders. These evil capitalists were known for stealing widow's homes for personal profit. Yet, the widow saw God behind the scenes.

While unrighteous capitalists were engaged in shady practices, God's work still had to be done. She gave more generously than most.[121] The same could be said of the business world. While it is often inhabited by evil capitalists, the righteous capitalist will not get discouraged but continue to be generous.

Righteous Capitalism Money Can't Buy

Bribery is common form of corruption in our world. It starts small as a mere tip for service and grows large to perks, sweetheart deals, kickbacks, secret commissions, stock options, campaign contributions, gifts and political corruption. Some countries are better known as *kleptocracies* because they are ruled by thieves who engage in government embezzlement.

Commercial drug sales people who buy lunch for a local doctor's staff and give kickbacks for heavy prescription of certain drugs are not much different. They have bought doctors. Commercial bribery is widespread in both legal and illegal forms. Sports corruption is also well-known.

Not so well-known is religious corruption. Simon, a sorcerer thought that he could buy the gift of God with money.[122] A major cause of the *Protestant Reformation* was the financial scandal associated with selling of indulgences to raise money to build *Saint Peter's* in Rome and other such corruption in the western church.[123] [124]

The ethical businessperson owes loyalty to one person only, God. The virtuous executive does not do shady deals. The righteous capitalist does not take bribes. The righteous capitalist is not going to compromise doing the right thing for 30 pieces of silver.

Righteous Capitalism not Hoarding

How does someone become a billionaire without hoarding? Is it even possible? Obviously some inherit, but those who accumulate, why have they not shared their fortunes with the needy? If they had, there would be no billions accumulated. Hoarding is not something that a righteous capitalist engages in. It hurts the hoarder and ruins their heirs. Take the example of a large retailer who was loved by his employees. After his death, his children had no compassion on the poor, lived in sickening opulence, better than royalty, while they deprived their employees of previously held benefits and lowered pay rates to working-poor levels. Righteous capitalists do not hoard, are self-sacrificing and provide a righteous inheritance for their children.[125]

The charitable capitalist does not lay up treasure for selfish reasons on earth where moth and rust corrupt and where thieves break in and steal. The righteous capitalist lays up treasures in heaven, by giving to Christ in the hungry, thirsty, stranger, naked, sick and imprisoned.[126] Moths and rust cannot destroy such treasures. Thieves cannot rob us of what we have freely given away.[127]

Righteous Capitalism no False Gods

Righteous capitalists use gold for righteous purposes. They do not use it to build useless idols.[128] We have our modern idols, but why did ancient people build literal idols? They saw them as saving them from crop failure or other material problems.

Our modern idols are no different. We see them as providing salvation. Politically we look to the left or the right. God warns us to obey him and not turn to the left or right.[129] Look straight ahead and do not swerve to the left or right.[130]Rather than waste money on a political party, put it to godly use.

Money becomes and idol. Yet the righteous capitalist knows that we cannot serve God and money.[131]

In the parable of *Lazarus and the Rich Man*,[132] it was the poor beggar who had a name. Even though later writers gave him the name Dives, it is made up. The original story gave the rich man no name. This is the exact opposite of popular thinking. The unrighteous capitalist wants a name for self and the poor beggar remains nameless.

This also contradicts the popular bigotry that the poor just need to get a job. Some cannot. Lazarus was dumped at the gate of the rich man. The original wording shows that he was incapable of moving himself there and his only option was to beg. The rich man's hard heart landed him in hell, but God took care of Lazarus and he was received into heaven.

Another modern idol is the god of pride.[133] Paul the Apostle instructed Timothy to preach against pride among the wealthy and to warn them against trusting in their riches. Wealth is deceptive. Look at the faces of pride among some well-known wealthy people. See their example and thinking that they are so much better than others. It is a drug that is hard to withdraw from. It is also living a lie.

Humility is not faked. It is just a reality check. Those who have pride have not come to reality. They do not see how weak they really are. Righteous capitalists see the reality of human frailty. They are not fooled by money, but put their trust in God.

Righteous Capitalism is Generous

The things of God are free. The righteous capitalist knows that the best things in life cannot be bought with money, and that generous giving is a wonderful blessing. God sets the pace by offering his bounties without price.[134]

Jesus gave the example of hiring day laborers for a job and giving generously.[135] How many employees today follow this example?

Righteous Capitalism Invests

Jesus invested in his students. He could have preached and not invested in the future of his work after his death, but instead he took along an expensive and extensive entourage of men and woman so as to teach them, so that they could carry on his work afterwards.[136] The most important investment of all is people.

In many small businesses it is a son or daughter who carries on after their parents die. While family relationships are important, the child is not always the best to carry on a business. Sometimes it is an "adopted" child, an apprentice or a loyal assistant. However successors are chosen, they are invested in over years and that investment is expensive and extensive.

Righteous Capitalism Rewards

In the *Parable of the Pounds* is also a lesson in investment and reward for the righteous capitalist.[137] Financial responsibility was distributed equally to employees, but not everyone produced. Those who produced more were given a greater reward and those who did not produce at all were punished. This is a law of equal opportunity, not a law of equal pay for the diligent as well as the lazy. It was a meritocracy, reward for diligence. It was not an excuse for greed.

In the similar *Parable of the Talents*,[138] different amounts were given out. In this case, financial responsibility was not distributed equally but according to each man's different abilities. This is a law of opportunity according to aptitude. Again we notice that this was not a law of equal pay for the diligent as well as the lazy. It was a meritocracy, reward for production. It was not an excuse for greed.

Righteous Capitalism releases Debts

In the *Parable of the Two Debtors*[139] Jesus explained that sin is a debt and forgiveness of sin is forgiveness of a debt. However, there is also a valuable financial lesson here for righteous capitalists. Forgiveness of debt is good for business. It engenders good relations.

In the *Parable of the Unmerciful Servant*[140] Jesus taught of the failure to forgive debt. Righteous capitalists have compassion on their fellow human beings. When we fail to forgive debt, we fail to see the greater debt that we owe. God has given us everything that we own. He can reclaim it at any moment that he desires. He graciously continues to allow us to enjoy what he has given, but if he detects injustice and greed, there is nothing stopping him from taking it all away from us again.

More importantly, we must forgive each other and show mercy from our hearts.

Goals of Righteous Capitalism

Love

A righteous capitalist has the main goals of *loving God and loving neighbor*. Loving God comes first, but is impossible unless we also love our neighbors.

Relieve and Restore

The good capitalist also engages in *relief* and *restoration*. Such an honest business broker realizes that it is "important to attend to the market's harmful consequences since it is the poor who often have to endure them."[141]

The righteous capitalist will operate his or her business within the community in such a manner as to lift up those who are downtrodden relieve their suffering and seek ways to restore them to their proper place as contributing members of society.

Imperfect Capitalism

Let's go back for a minute to the discussion of clothing which we had at the very beginning. An item of clothing may have been produced by slave labor, environmental contamination or other unrighteous working conditions. What if the company selling the clothing engages in some unethical business practices? Are we then responsible to investigate the source of every item of clothing that we buy? That would be impractical. We simply cannot become world police officers investigating the morality of everyone that we do business with.

What about wages? Righteous capitalists who are also "conscientious employers may want to pay their workers a living wage. However, they are constrained by the workings of the market. Should they pay such wages, their cost of production would increase substantially, and they would have to face the predicament of either raising their prices (and driving themselves out of the market) or sustaining large financial losses. Either choice is unappealing; both in fact would lead to the closure of their businesses, to the detriment of the employees themselves who would suddenly find themselves unemployed."[142]

The descriptions in this book of righteous capitalism may seem overwhelming. It may seem like an impossibly tall order, unattainable by mere mortals. None of us will be perfectly faultless capitalists. That's impossible. What are we imperfect capitalists supposed to do when we fail to live up to such high ideals? How are we supposed to look at ourselves in the mirror in the morning knowing that important business decisions may ruin lives? How can we capitalists who seek to be righteous face those unrighteous parts of our lives?

There is a misunderstanding among some religious people that human beings can become faultless. It is wrong. The passage that says to "be perfect"[143] actually means to be spiritually mature. A spiritually mature person knows that sinless perfection in humanity is impossible, and we need to become mature enough to understand that. Perfectionists live with unrealistic expectations.

Grace and Forgiveness

The twin traits of grace and forgiveness are necessary for righteous capitalism. The righteous capitalist knows that absolute moral perfection is impossible among mere mortals. Righteous capitalists operate in a dirty field filled with corruption and shady deals. He or she learns to forgive others around for their imperfect decisions, and even the wrongs done by fellow business operators to them. Just as importantly, virtuous business people know their own foibles and learn to ask forgiveness and move on.

How can we capitalists forgive ourselves and our fellows? There is a simple answer, if we ask for God's forgiveness then we must also forgive ourselves because God has. If we, the ones attempting to be honorable entrepreneurs have sinned, we just need to get over it. We have all done wrong things. If our fellow capitalists have transgressed against us then we must forgive them as God has forgiven us.

In one of history's remarkable quotes, Jesus forgave on the cross before people were even sorry their sins.[144] Like him, we must pray, "Father forgive them, they know not what they do." Learn to forgive those who have wronged us before they even come to their senses. Most of the time, none of us really knows the harm (or the good) that our actions may have caused. We don't know what we are doing.

We human beings cannot handle matters with faultless perfection. It is impossible to do business in perfect blamelessness. We just do the best we can and thank God for his forgiveness. Ignore those co-workers who do not forgive us and get on with the job.

Better a faulty capitalist who is at least trying to be righteous than an unrighteous capitalist who doesn't even care.

Righteous Capitalism with Humility

Righteous capitalists know that we humans make mistakes, sometimes big ones. We must be willing to enter a world where we know that we will make mistakes and sometimes hurt others. But we do so in humility, not placing ourselves above our fellow human beings and thankful when others forgive us for our many faults.[145]

Righteous capitalists know that we are not saviors of the world, yet we try to follow the one who is and bring a measure of material salvation to others as we have opportunity.

Capital Ideas

Application is always a process of debate and varying opinions. Let's explore some possibilities by asking some important questions. What is righteous compensation for a CEO? What is righteous compensation for an ordinary worker? What is a just price for goods and services? What is a righteous inheritance? Can business be too big to be righteous?

The Main Benchmark

There is one benchmark for every capital decision. It is a measure that sets the standard that every venture ought to be measured against: Does this show love to God and neighbor? How does that kind of thinking work on the ground?

For instance, if we own a country store that is mile from any public restroom do we put in a toilet for the convenience of customers or is it just too much of a hassle for us? The selfish capitalist will say that a restroom is an inconvenience to any business. There is the constant cleaning every few hours and the occasional bad mess to clean up. Some in the public will just abuse the privilege and write graffiti on the restroom walls or break things. None of that answers the question: does this show love to God and neighbor?

Of course, the answer is obvious. If we want to say that a restroom is inconvenient, maybe our customers will just find us to be too inconvenient because if they need to go to the toilet, and some customers do need to visit that room regularly, then perhaps the store in the other direction is better to shop at. Not every business decision is made by the bottom line. Perhaps it will cost a few more dollars to provide convenient facilities for customers than is returned by a slight increase in traffic, but that's not most important question. Does it show love to God and neighbor?

A just compensation

CEO's are either righteous or unrighteous kings of industry. Unrighteous CEO's feed on their employees like scavengers feed on carrion. Such vulture capitalism is the height of selfishness. Righteous CEO's are givers not takers. They give their lives not just for their own families, but also for their extended family of employees. They are caring shepherds who know that their life's job is to look after not just a faceless list of names, but each and every employee and their families as well. How does this relate to pay scale?

Unions can also be very greedy, expecting too much from employers or destroying property and causing economic problems for the larger community. Certainly, unionism may be a needed balance to the greed that often exists at the top, but union thuggery can be just as bad as executive thuggery. Two wrongs don't make a right. Tied in with righteous executive compensation is righteous employee compensation.

On the one extreme are grossly excessive CEO pay scales. For instance, the CEO of a large bank contracted for a quarter billion dollar package and a few years later played the game of outward appearances by taking a $1 salary during hard times. The whole think stunk of hypocrisy and executive muscle when employees were forced to forego bonuses and pay raises, but in the end the CEO still made out like a bandit with a grossly excessive golden parachute.

On the other hand, it is a shame to see businesses go bankrupt because employees are unwilling to negotiate a lower pay and benefits package during recessions. We must all make sacrifices in hard times and shooting the goose that lays the golden eggs is never a smart move.

Another extreme might be those who executives who take nothing from their businesses, either because they don't need the money or in some cases have taken a vow of poverty. What a blessing it must be to have an income stream that is independent of the business and allows the luxury of returning all profits to the business and its personnel.

The most extreme of all must be monks who can run very lucrative businesses but take a vow of poverty. They live without such gross excesses of luxury as personal jets, yachts, limousines, mansions. They live without even everyday luxuries like a marriage and home. They live simple, uncomplicated lives and give any profits to the needy. Is that the standard that CEO's should strive for? Are there CEO's who live simple lives and have no need of luxury? It may be better not to make vows of celibacy or poverty, because life changes. However, the personal choice of poverty is certainly a very honorable one, even for those who are not monks.

Righteous CEO's certainly have the right to take a salary, but at what level? For CEO's who choose to take a salary, what is a righteous income? What about ordinary employees? How should they be paid? Should there be a big difference between the pay of an executive and an employee on the line? Some more principles might help make that very difficult decision.

Principle of double honorarium

What is a righteous pay level? The principle of double honorarium[146] for those who do well is a good place to start. A laborer or manager who directs the affairs of a business well deserves double honor and that is equated with double pay, especially those who teach. What? Ought employees to teach? Why not? Why do we have employees who hold back their fellow employees by refusing to share vital knowledge which would increase team performance?

Let's theoretically call this principle of double honorarium a two-tiered pay scale: maybe minimum wage and double or perhaps to be generous, a multiple of minimum wage and double that. In such a two-tier system of pay how do we evaluate who gets what pay?

Could we start everyone off at tier one and create a system of incentives whereby their pay grows to double over time according to a whole array of factors? Could diligence, efficiency, ability, teamwork, harmony and attitude be factors? Could it be a peer-review system, an anonymous check list done by peers as well as managers so as to provide the best possible perspective and incentive? Could it be a fair and equitable incentive system that gives everyone a level playing field with the possibility of periodic bonuses depending on company profitability?

There are many possibilities. This is a good place to start, but it is just that, a start of the discussion. There are other principles to consider.

The One Percent Principle

In ancient Israel a tenth of the people's income was given to the Levites. A tenth of that was given to the high priest.[147] Notice that this was not the salary of the high priest, but the entire budget for the priest. This budgeted one percent for the executive office is a good principle of the cost of doing business at the top.

The 1% budget even included the best things for the high priest, and makes no apology about it. Is there a difference between this and the compensation paid at the widget factory? That is an open question. CEO's are not high priests, but there are some parallels perhaps worthy of discussion.

The principle of clan-sized business

Clan-sized family businesses create within them an automatic and sustainable welfare system. All can be cared for because they are not just employees. They are family. Sacrifice for the business is not just the lot of the clan's heads or the employees. Everyone must pull together and everyone must contribute as they are able.

One of the great crimes of our modern industrial system has been the separation of children and mothers and fathers from each other. Our families are a mess. In a family business there need be no artificial separation of family members to avoid favoritism as exists in large corporate situations. The clan model has many benefits and can be a way to at least partly heal the harm done by the industrial age.

One of the reasons that many executives love big business is because they can make a lot of money. Big businesses are often as inefficient as national governments, but top executives can extract from them enormous salaries.

The economy of ancient Israel was a model for the world to learn from. It was neither meant to be communism nor an example of greedy and destructive vulture capitalism. It was a model of righteous capitalism and was based on clan-sized, family businesses. Each clan or family was a business. They engaged primarily in farming and small manufacturing.

How do we translate that to today's economy? Is not our economy grossly inefficient when we ship parts from all over the globe to assemble? Is it not ridiculous to buy bananas from South America and Oranges from Florida and Basa fish from Vietnam and wine from France, when maybe our bodies are designed to eat more indigenous foods and our economy would be vastly improved if most of our needs could be produced locally?

Granted, CEO's may make less money if they broke their companies up into smaller businesses, but would the economy improve? Would the lives of ordinary people improve? Would the market be freer and less monopolistic? Would a country set up on a majority of clan-sized businesses be better off? Small business is the main driver of the economy even today, not inefficient big business. That is the model that God gave to ancient Israel. Does it have application and merit in today's world?

Principles of Righteous Inheritance

When the heirs of a big box retailer inherited an incredible fortune, was that a just inheritance? The heirs have not treated their employees as well as their father did, but instead built themselves opulent castles and squeezed their employees to the point of breaking. They no longer pay a just health benefit and have lowered wages to poverty levels. Such unjust CEO's are the epitome of the vulture capitalist.

Several wise billionaires have commented that they will give away most of their fortunes before they die, leaving only a few million for their children to inherit. Whether or not their accumulation was righteous capitalism in the first place, their decision is a righteous one. Repentance later in life is better than no repentance at all.

A righteous inheritance considers the contribution of future generations to society as a whole. Business inheritance goes to the most competent to continue that business in a righteous manner. That person may not always the most closely related.

The kings of ancient Israel and the kings and queens of Britain have a similar story to tell.

101

Most were awfully bad rulers. Inheritance does not guarantee good leadership.

The reset principle

Communism is sometimes confused with redistribution, but that is a misunderstanding. Communism was theft of private property by government, not the redistribution of private ownership. Ancient Israel had a policy of redistribution that was much different than communism.

The economy was set up on an agrarian model very different than any in history. Everyone except the religious class had an inheritance in the land of approximately equal value. When people lost their farms due to debt or war, the system was designed to reset the economy back to its default mode. There was no opportunity for people to accumulate ever larger parts of the national pie. Every 7 and 50 years, the reset button was pushed and the land was redistributed back to its original owners.

How do we apply the reset principle to today? We are not an agrarian society? Might we need to consider something along the lines of equal access to education? Is taxing the super-rich fair so as to make sure they do not take an unfair percentage of the economy? What is too rich? Should we mandate the breakup of businesses if they become too large? What is too large? The reset principle is actually two principles in one: relief and restoration.

Principles of Relief and Restoration

In loving our weaker neighbor, the main goals are relief and restoration. Let's discuss this in a little greater detail this time. These two words summarize the great economic principles that God gave to ancient Israel.[148] How can we today relieve and restore those who have fallen on hard times? To what should we restore them? Is restoration to a previously held low level of existence all that is needed or would the righteous capitalist be expected to restore them to a higher ideal of what life should have been like?

Does this mean that the righteous capitalist will consider ways that employees can be helped to find decent housing and affordable health care? Ought righteous capitalists to be engaged in the education business either on site or elsewhere? Ought apprenticeships to be something that a righteous capitalist creates? How can we help employees become all that they can be? How can we serve others in such a manner that they can become fully contributing members of the community?

The Principle of Sacrifice

Ought righteous capitalists to think about making the ultimate business sacrifice by finding ways to help their own employees become their competitors? Now that is the hardest question of all.

However, every human being is called to make sacrifices for others. That is what civilized society is all about. Righteous capitalism is what makes the difference between a society that operates on the laws of the jungle and a truly civilized society. Without self-sacrifice we are not better than beasts. With self-sacrifice we live like God.

Real Efficiency

When we speak of efficiency, we are often concerned only with the bottom line, money. Money is only one of many considerations. What is real efficiency? Ought real efficiency to also consider the employees' family lives? For the sake of the almighty dollar, are we ruining marriages and harming the environment? Can a business be truly efficient if it is not efficiently contributing good in every facet of society?

Is not real efficiency a macro-study, rather than a micro-study of just economic factors? Must not real efficiency then begin with love of God and love of neighbor, relieving and restoring those in need? May we then and only then say that we have begun to understand righteous capitalism?

Endnotes

---

[1]

http://www.investorwords.com/694/capital.ht
ml#ixzz2BpqKzHAo

[2]

http://www.huffingtonpost.com/2012/11/27/b
est-education-in-the-wor_n_2199795.html

[3] Matthew 25:31-46

[4] Rynell, Amy. CAUSES OF POVERTY: Findings
from Recent Research. The Heartland Alliance.
Mid-America Institute on Poverty. 2008.

[5]

http://www.nytimes.com/2012/10/14/opinion/
sunday/the-self-destruction-of-the-1-
percent.html?pagewanted=all&src=ISMR_AP_L
O_MST_FB&_r=1&

[6] Mark 12:28-34

[7] Butler, Smedley. War is a Racket. Booklet.
1933

[8] War is a Racket

[9] War is a Racket

[10] Butler, Smedley. Interventionism. Speech.
1933.

[11] Barrera, Albino. Economic Compulsion And
Christian Ethics. n.p.: Cambridge University
Press, 2005. eBook Collection (EBSCOhost).
Web. 23 Nov. 2012. P. xi.

[12] Economic Compulsion and Christian Ethics.
p. xii.

[13] Hebrews 11

[14] Romans 15:1

[15] Economic Compulsion and Christian Ethics.
p. 56.

---

[16] Economic Compulsion and Christian Ethics. p. 74

[17] Economic Compulsion and Christian Ethics. p. 110

[18] Luke 3:7-18

[19] http://abcnews.go.com/WNT/story?id=2743456&page=1#.UNHt1W88CSo

[20] Freeland, Chrystia. 2012. Plutocrats: The Rise of the New Global Super-Rich and the Fall of Everyone Else. New York: Penguin Group. p. 221

[21] Plutocrats. p. 141

[22] Plutocrats. p. 267

[23] http://www.nytimes.com/2012/10/14/opinion/sunday/the-self-destruction-of-the-1-percent.html?pagewanted=all&_r=0

[24] http://www.nytimes.com/2012/12/06/world/europe/oligarchs-play-a-role-in-greeces-economic-troubles.html?emc=eta1&_r=0

[25] Plutocrats. p. 127

[26] Plutocrats. p. 96

[27] Plutocrats. p. 205

[28] Plutocrats. p. 250

[29] Plutocrats. p. 45

[30] Plutocrats. p. 256

[31] Plutocrats. p. 226

[32] Plutocrats. p. 134

[33] Plutocrats. p. 189

[34] Proverbs 28:25

[35] Psalm 10:1-4

36 http://www.newadvent.org/fathers/1801010.htm
37 Proverbs 1:19
38 http://www.biblestudytools.com/commentaries/matthew-henry-concise/ecclesiastes/4.html
39 Ecclesiastes 4:7-8
40 http://www.sacred-texts.com/bib/cmt/clarke/pro015.htm
41 Proverbs 15:27
42 James 5:1-3
43 Proverbs 29:4
44 http://www.biblestudytools.com/commentaries/wesleys-explanatory-notes/isaiah/isaiah-56.html
45 Isaiah 56:11
46 Jeremiah 22:16-18
47 Ezekiel 33:30-32
48 Matthew 23:24-26; Luke 11:37-41
49 Luke 12:14-21
50 Mark 7:20-23
51 Romans 1:29
52 1 Corinthians 5:9-11
53 Ephesians 4:19
54 Ephesians 5:3-6; Colossians 3:4-6
55 1 Timothy 3:3, 8
56 Luke 3:14
57 Micah 3:10-12
58 http://www.cauxroundtable.org/
59 Plutocrats. p. 50
60 Plutocrats. p. 82

[61] Plutocrats. p. 91

[62] Plutocrats. p. 125

[63] Matthew 22:34-40

[64] Matthew 25:31-46

[65] Genesis 4:9

[66] Matthew 22:39

[67] Matthew 22:34-40

[68] Ecclesiastes 11:1-3

[69] Matthew 25:31-46

[70] Rynell, Amy. CAUSES OF POVERTY: Findings from Recent Research. The Heartland Alliance. Mid-America Institute on Poverty. 2008.

[71] Proverbs 21:25-26

[72] Matthew 19:16-28

[73] Hagner, D. A. (2002). Vol. 33B: Word Biblical Commentary: Matthew 14-28. Word Biblical Commentary (562). Dallas: Word, Incorporated.

[74] France, R. T. The Gospel of Matthew New International Commentary on the New Testament. NICNT, Wm. B. Eerdmans Publishing Co., 2007

[75] Matthew 19:21

[76] Luke 3:1-6

[77] Luke 12:13-21

[78] John 10:10-18

[79] John 10:11-18

[80] 1 Timothy 6:17

[81] 1 Timothy 6:17-18

[82] Acts 10:35

[83] Exodus 22:25

[84]

http://www.christnotes.org/commentary.php?c

om=mhc&b=3&c=25
[85] Leviticus 25:35-38
[86] Deuteronomy 23:19-20
[87] Nehemiah 5:1-11
[88] http://www.mbda.gov/node/438
[89] Psalm 112:4-6
[90] Ezekiel 18:12-14
[91] Luke 6:30-36
[92] Proverbs 22:7
[93] Exodus 21:2–6; Deuteronomy 15:12–18
[94] Economic Compulsion and Christian Ethics. p. 115
[95] Economic Compulsion and Christian Ethics. p. 116
[96] Proverbs 3:13-18
[97] Proverbs 16:16
[98] Proverbs 11:28
[99] Numbers 35:31
[100] 1 Samuel 8:2-4
[101] Proverbs 11:1
[102] Proverbs 10:16
[103] Proverbs 13:11
[104] Habakkuk 2:8-13
[105] 2 Pet 2:3
[106] Jude 11
[107] Ezekiel 7:18-20
[108] Matthew 19:16-30
[109] Luke 3:1-6
[110] Luke 12
[111] http://en.wikipedia.org/wiki/Just_price
[112] Ecclesiastes 5:9-11
[113] 1 Timothy 6:10
[114] 2 Timothy 3:1-2

[115] Hebrews 13:5
[116] Malachi 3:8-12
[117] Deuteronomy 14:28; 26:12
[118] Deuteronomy 14:22-27
[119]
http://www.pdegraaf.com/articles/joysoftithing.pdf
[120] Matthew 26:9; Mark 14:5
[121] Mark 12:41-44
[122] Acts 8:9-25
[123]
http://en.wikipedia.org/wiki/Protestant_Reformation#Corruption
[124]
http://www.theopedia.com/Protestant_Reformation
[125] Ecclesiastes 5:13-15
[126] Matthew 25:31-46
[127] Matthew 6:19-21
[128] Isaiah 46:4-6
[129] Deuteronomy 5:32
[130] Proverbs 4:27
[131] Matthew 6:24
[132] Luke 16:19-31
[133] 1 Timothy 6:17-19
[134] Isaiah 55:1-2
[135] Matthew 20:13-15
[136] Matthew 20:14-28
[137] Luke 19:11-27
[138] Matthew 25:14-30
[139] Luke 7:36-50
[140] Matthew 18:23-35
[141] Economic Compulsion and Christian Ethics.

p. xiv.
[142] Economic Compulsion and Christian Ethics.
p. 23.
[143] Matthew 5:48
[144] Luke 23:34
[145] Proverbs 15:33; 18:12; 29:23
[146] Isaiah 61:7; 1 Timothy 5:17
[147] Numbers 18:25-29
[148] Economic Compulsion and Christian Ethics.
p. 84-85.

www.ingramcontent.com/pod-product-compliance
Lightning Source LLC
Chambersburg PA
CBHW022025170526
45157CB00003B/1365